Be an eco hero

At home

Sue Barraclough

W

FRANKLIN WATTS

LONDON•SYDNEY

First published in 2010
by Franklin Watts

Copyright © Franklin Watts 2010

Franklin Watts
338 Euston Road
London NW1 3BH

Franklin Watts Australia
Level 17/207 Kent Street
Sydney, NSW 2000

Series editor: Sarah Peutrill
Art director: Jonathan Hair
Design: Robert Walster, Big Blu Design
Illustrator: Gary Swift

Dewey number: 640

ISBN 978 0 7496 9336 7

Printed in China

Franklin Watts is a division of
Hachette Children's Books, an
Hachette UK company.
www.hachette.co.uk

Credits: Anyka/istockphoto: 14bl. Timur Arbaev/istockphoto: 14cr. Gerald Barnard/istockphoto: 16r. Todd Bates/Istockphoto: 23c. Martin Carlsson/istockphoto: 11b. Tye Carnelli/istockphoto: 24b. Yvonne Chamberlain/istockphoto: 6t. Kimberley Deprey/istockphoto: 21t. Elena Elisseeva/Shutterstock: 19cl. Elnur/Shutterstock: 25l. EML/Shutterstock: 10r. Mandy Godbehear/istockphoto: 18b. Kim Gunkel/istockphoto: 13bl. Hallgerd/Shutterstock: 19b. Andrew Hill/istockphoto: 15br. J Hindman/Shutterstock: 16l. Justin Horrocks/istockphoto: 13tc. Image Source/Corbis: 8t. istockphoto: 23b. Maksym Kravtsov/istockphoto: 15bl. Andrey Kuzmin/Shutterstock: 10l. Edyta Luiek/istockphoto: 19t. Mona Mekela/istockphoto: 25cl. Jim Mills/istockphoto: 23t. Monkey Business Images/Shutterstock: 19cr. Juriah Mosin/Shutterstock: 6b, 13br. Ramplett/istockphoto: front cover, 25cr. RAT87/Shutterstock: 25b. Morley Read/istockphoto: 9. runamock/istockphoto: 17. Nassyrov Ruslan/Shutterstock: 13tl. Jorge Salcedo/istockphoto: 14tr. Kristian Sekulic/istockphoto: 8b. Nina Shannon/istockphoto: 15t. sonyat/istockphoto: 22. Studio Araminta/Shutterstock: 25tr. Tihis/Shutterstock: 13tr. Deniz Unlusu/istockphoto: 18tl. Wishlist Images: 7, 20, 26, 27. Feng Yu/Shutterstock: 25tc. Sergey Zavalnyuk/istockphoto: 21b. Every attempt has been made to clear copyright. Should there be any inadvertent omission please apply to the publisher for rectification.

Contents

Words in **bold** are in the glossary on page 28.

Find out ways to help your planet in this book and become an eco hero like me!

At home

Our homes are full of things that use **energy**. We use **gas** for cooking and for heating our homes. We use **electricity** for lights and to make machines work.

We use water in lots of ways around the home too. We use it for baths, showers, toilets and cleaning cars.

Think of all the things we have in our homes, from furniture to **packaging**, TVs to clothes. All these things are made using energy.

Using energy

We all use a lot of energy such as electricity in our homes every day. Think of all the things we do that use electricity.

All around you there are many other homes using energy too. So if we all save energy, it can make a big difference.

Why Save energy?

Most energy is **generated** by burning **fossil fuels,** such as coal. Electricity is generated in **power stations** and travels along power lines like these to our homes.

Power lines

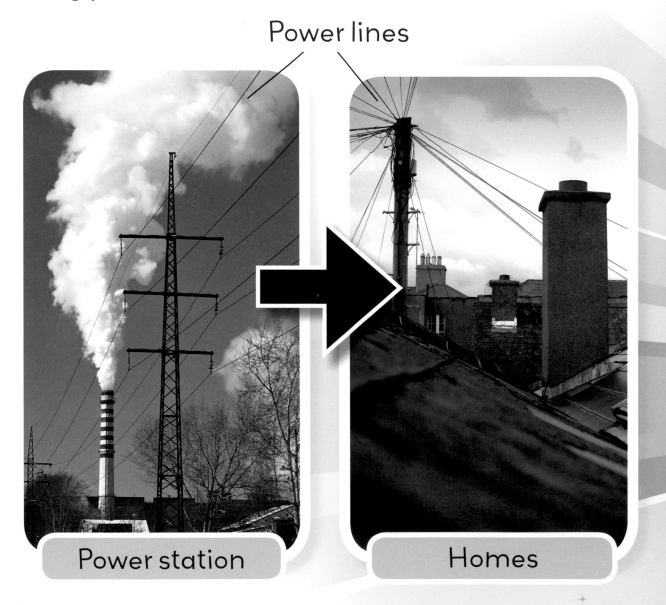

Power station

Homes

Fossil fuels will not last forever and we are using them up quickly. Burning fossil fuels also fills the air with dangerous gases.

You can be an eco hero by using less energy. For example, you can help to choose light bulbs that are energy **efficient**. This means they use less energy and last much longer.

Saving energy

There are lots of easy ways to save energy.

Be an eco hero by:

- Wearing warm clothes and turning down heating to save energy.
- Switching off lights in empty rooms.
- Not leaving TVs, CD players and other items on standby.
- Reading a book or playing a game instead of watching TV.
- Switching off and unplugging mobile phone chargers when not in use.

Unplug

Switch off

Turn off

Wear warm clothes

Read a book

Using water

We all use a lot of water in our homes every day. Think about all the things you do every day that use water.

Washing hands

Flushing the toilet

Drinking water

Can you think of ways to use less water?

Cleaning teeth

Boiling the kettle

Watering the garden

15

Why save water?

Water falls from the sky as rain. It is stored in lakes and **reservoirs**. It is cleaned and pumped along pipes to taps in our homes. This takes energy.

Rainwater

Tap

Clean, fresh water is **precious**. But, the number of people who live on the planet is growing. We all have to share the supply of water. When there is not enough rain some places can get **droughts**.

If we all save water, it can make a big difference. You can be an eco hero by saving water at home.

Saving water

Be an eco hero by:

• Asking an adult to mend dripping taps. A dripping tap wastes four **litres** of water every day.

• Using a bucket to wash the car, not a hose.

• Using a watering can, not a hose to water plants.

• Filling the dishwasher: one full load uses less water than several small ones.

• Not leaving the tap running while you brush your teeth.

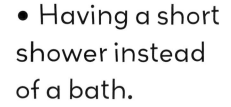

• Having a short shower instead of a bath.

Why reduce, reuse, recycle?

Everything we buy and use is made using energy. Glass, plastic, paper, food, toys, clothes, books and machines are all made using energy and **raw materials.**